T0113589

Lovely

Joyce

ALAN HINES

ISBN: 978-1-6987-0750-1 (sc)
ISBN: 978-1-6987-0751-8 (hc)
ISBN: 978-1-6987-0749-5 (e)

Trafford rev. 05/21/2021

 www.trafford.com

North America & international
toll-free: 844-688-6899 (USA & Canada)
fax: 812 355 4082

Books of poetry already published by Alan Hines

1. Reflections of Love
2. Thug Poetry Volume 1
3. The Words I Spoke
4. Joyce
5. Constant Visions
6. Red Ink of Blood
7. Beauty of Love
8. Reflections of Love Volume 2
9. Reflections of Love Volume 3
10. True Love Poetry
11. Visionary.
12. Love Volume 1
13. This is Love
14. This Is Love Volume 2
15. This Is Love Volume 3
16. Garden of Love
17. Reflections of Love Volume 4
18. Reflections of Love Volume 5
19. Reflections of Love Volume 6
20. Reflections of Love Volume 7
21. Reflections of Love Volume 8
22. Reflections of Love Volume 9
23. Reflections of Love Volume 10
24. Godly Tendecies
25. Permanemt Blood Stain Volume 1
26. Permanemt Blood Stain Volume 2
27. Reflections of Love Volume 11
28. Reflections of Love Volume 12
29. Admiration of Love Volumes 1 and 2

Urban Novel already published by Alan Hines,

Upcoming books of poetry by Alan Hines,

1. Reflections of Love Volume 3
2. This is Love (Volume 1, 2, and 3)
3. Founded Love (Volume 1, 2, and 3)
4. True Love (Volume 1, 2, and 3)
5. Love (Endless Volumes)
6. Tormented Tears (Volume 1, 2, and 3)
7. A Inner Soul That Cried (Volume 1, 2, and 3)
8. Visionary (Endless Volumes)
9. A Seed That Grew (Volume 1, 2, and, 3)
10. The Words I Spoke (Volume 2, and 3)
11. Scriptures (Volume 1, 2, and 3)
12. Revelations (volume 1, 2, and 3)
13. Destiny (Volume 1, 2, and 3)
14. Trials and Tribulations (Volume 1, 2, and 3)
15. IMMORTALITY (Volume 1,2, and 3)
16. My Low Spoken Words (Volume 1, 2, and 3)
17. Beauty Within (Volume 1, 2, and 3)
18. Red Ink of Blood (Volume 1, 2, and 3)
19. Destiny of Light (Jean Hines) (Volume 1, 2, and 3)
20. Deep Within (Volume 1, 2, and 3)
21. Literature (Volume 1, 2, and 3)
22. Silent Mind (Volume 1, 2, and 3)
23. Amor (Volume 1, 2, and 3)
24. Joyce (Volume 1, 2, and 3)
25. Lovely Joyce (Volume 1, 2, and 3)
26. Pink Lady (Volume 1, 2, and 3)
27. Mockingbird Lady (Volume 1, 2, and 3)

Upcoming non-fiction books by Alan Hines,

1. Time Versus Life
2. Timeless Jewels
3. The Essence of Time
4. Memoirs of My Life
5. In my Eyes To See
6. A Prisoner's Black History

Upcoming Urban Novels by Alan Hines,

1. Black Kings
2. Playerlistic
3. The Police
4. Scandalous Scandal
5. The West Side Rapist
6. Shattered Dreams
7. She Wrote Murder
8. Black Fonz
9. A Slow Form of Suicide
10. No Motherfucking Love
11. War Stories
12. Race against time
13. Ghetto Heros
14. Boss Pimps
15. Adolescents
16. In The Hearts of Men
17. Story Teller
18. Kidnapping
19. Mob Ties

Acknowledgements

Heavenly Father thank you for blessing me to live to see another day; thank you for all your many blessings which include me writing and being able to publish another book.

1. Raised

Above and beyond raised.
Love that was genuinely gave.
Descendants that gave birth to lives was made.
Never left us alone,
always had a place to stay.
Loving, and missing you more,
and more each day.
Memories shall never fade.
The love you gave, in
paradise your soul was raised.

2. Legacy of Living

Life that was giving.
A lovely mother,
lovely children.
What a wonderful feeling.
To be loved, to be living.
Through seeded children,
you shall always be loved,
legacy of living.

3. Fly Til The End

Fly til the end of time.
We all living to die.
Enjoy the happiness,
sometimes pain will come tears to cry.
Through it all we gotta stay strong,
and give life a try.

Fly til the end of time.

4. Above The Sky

Mom, it seems as if I can see you above the clouds
in the sky.
Mom guess what, I sign more contracts,
books of poetry, and one of non-fiction of truthfulness
no lie.
When I'm home alone I shed tears of why.
Around your kids, and grandkids you know
I shall never ever let them see me cry.
Things aren't and will never be the same,
casket never wanted to see the inside.
Just wish you were still at home so I could stop by.
In peace in the Haevens wings to fly,
fly mom high above the sky.

5. Ruler Of My World

I see your reflection in waters of midnight lakes
within this world.
My diamond my pearl.
Birthed me, made it warmful in this cold world.
Could see your face would always be present in
times of despair, turmoil.
Times of less, made it happen, blessed,
a continious swirl.
Loved your seeds shared your world,
a crown, a ruler,
she ruled the world.

6. You

A representation of you.
A reflection of you.
Everything I have is because of you.
My lady hero, my love unto.
My love overwhelmed as always due.
The trueness of true.
My lady above the skies,
my lady sky blue, you.

7. Believe In Love

Believe in love,
believe in light.
God will shine his light.
An awakening in paradise.

8. Memorable Memories

Memorable memories.
In my slumbers, and visions is all I see.
From birth, your first seed.
The last of a dying breed.
Once Earthly lady enjoy yourself
being Heavenly freed.
Indeed memories never cease to proceed.
Love to be, as I'll make you proud
of me.
Melodies harmony, memories.

9. Feeling It

I'm feeling it from my head to my toes.
Feeling it never wanted to let go.
Feeling it mom I love you so.

10. Rising In The Sun

Rising in the sun.
As birth become, begotten son.
Made my childhood lovely and fun.
Honored to be thou son.
Distinguished woman my numero uno, my number one.
I see reflections of you through the lake shores,
that glistens your smile through the rising of the sun.
An angelic angel you arouse to paradise to become.
Shine forever, out shine the rising of the sun.

11. Prevail

Ringing of bells.
Wish you well.
Fly high prevail.

12. I Can't Believe

I can't believe this
day finally become.
Wish you could've lived in the form
of flesh,
forever more to come.
Peace atleast, sleep tight mom.

13. My Lovely Queen

She had me when she was only sixteen.
A lovely young lady a beauty queen.
Love me more than things really seemed.
Been there through it all when
low income dried up streams.
The woman that gave me life to dream.
Upon judgement day you shall
inherit eternal life,
meet the king of kings.
My lovely lady my beauty queen.

14. Never Wanted To See

Never wanted to see you leave.
Not in front of the audience,
but in my heart, mind, soul, I shall forever
grieve.
Your life gave me life nourishment to feed.
If you had it I was never in need.
My lovely lady forever to be.
My love, my lovely lady Joyce
I never wanted to see you leave.
My whole hearted love shall forever bleed.

15. Memory Lane

In loving memory, I remember
almost everything as I float down memory lane.

I remember as a kid in snowy winter times
of Christmas you made it rain.
Wish I could hear your voice again.
I just love hearing your name.
It is a shame,
but Heaven gain.

16. Sweet Dreams

A shining sensational delight.
Gave me hope, shining lights, gave me this life.
Reached great heights.
Peacefully sleep, sweet dreams
throughout the dreams and nights.

17. Precious Lady

Precious lady.
Precious lady of living.
So wonderful, so forgiving.
Reach out to those in the projects
as if they was your own children.
Precious lady of giving.

18. Motherly Love Cast Angels

Motherly love cast angels from up above
be a guardian angel for those drowning
in floods.
Feed the hunger with food of love.
Be a shield from violence, a rehab for drugs.
Motherly love cast angels from up above
be our savior, savior of love.

19. 2515 W. Jackson

2515 W. Jackson.
Overlapping, relapsing heart
collapsing, love everlasting.
Back to the past missing you like action.
2515 W. Jackson.

20. Cute

She was cute in her eternal sleep,
but she looked better when she was alive
arouse I wish I pray I hope love floats.

21. Thanks To You

Thanks to you I write music for artist to sing
also poetry is my thing.
On Earth you gave birth to me as your
first born seeded king.
As a teenager you provided me with this
life to live live out my dreams.
To me you mean more than the world my angel
my motherly queen.
Rest in Heaven sleep tight
and sweet dreams.

22. Good Heart

Good heart.
Love never depart.
Offspring she'd never be apart;
would travel to the depths as astronauts far.
Loved genuinely accepting people through their flaws
of who they really are.
A marvelous star.

23. Lovely Mother

Lovely mother,
they'll never be no other,
not another.
Blessed to be your son,
blessed to be able to go futher.

24. Birth

White birds that fly from the palms
of my hand to the sky,
wishing this day had never become.
Love you, and miss you mom.
You from birth in which I come from.
Loving in sums,
praying and reading Psalms.
To the east I face, to the skies up my palms.
Memorable visions shall never fade, as since birth
they begun.

25. Best Of You

As you were, as you'll forever be,
memories.
You gave the best of you, wanted a better me.
Wanted me to forever be free.
Wanted me to get out live a little,
sights to see.
Said I'd make a good husband to my wife
when I decided to marry.
Poetry being read as my fingers caress
the piano's keys, sweet melodies.
Best it ever was, gave the best of you to me.

26. Rest

Rest, your bones, soul, your mind.
Love you more all the time.
Sleep mom we good the kids and grandkids fine.
Rest in peace ease your mind, above clouds
enchanting ray shine.
Rest in peace until the end of time.

Rest mom, rest your bones, soul, your mind.
Love of a lifetime.

27. A gift, A Gem

A gift a gem a love within.
A mother, and friend.
Time shall repeat itself with no end.
Thanks for it all, thanks for being a friend.

28. The One

The one and only, would
never leave me lonely.
Never phony.
Never be another, the one and only.

29. My Mother

My mother, my tooth fairy,
my Mrs. Clause, love she gave
me her all.

My mother my teacher, my guider,
my provider.

My mother my love my start,
fireworks, of firely sparks.

30. Love Unto

Love so many things I wish I
could tell you.
Thou shall prevail never fail you.
My love unto.
Sky blue.
Love, love unto.

31. Mommy

The love that came.
Came like a permenant stain.
Blessed me with life gave me my first name.
Around you from profanity I reframe.
My queen.

32. Mom I'll Love

Mom I'll Love you more
even when the king of kings
come down from his kingdom
to retrieve his souls galore.
Mom I'll love you more,
mom you wonderful, plus and more.

33. Essence of Time

Essence of time.
Love to body, soul, and mind.
No faded visions,
love all the time.
Love is of the essence.
Essence of time.

34. She Exercised

She exercised her freedom of speech,
it was her choice.
Her opinion she'd constantly voice.
Loved hearing her voice.
Lovely lady be free and rejoice.

The growth of seven seeds condensed moist.

The peoples choice this lovely
lady Joyce.

35. Flowered Lady

Blossom flowered lady thanks for the life you gave me.
Love positively, never a question of maybe.
Thanks for the way you raised me.
Roses, Daffodil, Lilies, flowered lady.

36. Revealed

Love revealed it.
Love never concealed it.
Perish but the love I can still feel it.

37. Memories In Time

Memories shall never fade in time.
You stay within our hearts and mind.
Wish you could be here within the changing of time.
Love the way you loved, the way you shine.

38. Everlasting

Everlasting.
Love long lasting.
Angels casting.
From artwork images of our queen,
with a Gold crown everlasting.

39. Love Beyond

Appreciate.
Congratulate.
Love beyond the coming of days.

40. As Much As We Need You

As much as we need you,
it's wonderful that you are in peace.
Love shall always increase.
From palms of our hands lovely white birds
fly to sky for you to meet.
Be at peace.

41. Love Feast

Love feast.
Love she.
Crush Satan dragon of the beast.

42. I Want To Go Home

I want to go home where it's
a love to call my own.

I want to go home where
my love as a kid lives on.

I want to go home to be,
a kid again in the privacy of my own room.

43. Dressed

Dressed in white veil.
I love you, and wish you well.

Dressed as the maid of honor,
for you I'll always honor.

Dressed in love to prevail,
I love you, and wish you well.

44. In Time Of

In time of need your love surely feeds.

In time of despair thanks for always being there.

In time of unpleasant circumstances, thanks
for being more than a friend.

45. To Be Loved

To be loved.
To be understood.
To be featured.
To be cherished.

46. Raised Me

My love lady.
The love you gave me.
The way you raised me.

47. Begun

Mom.
Love begun.
Birth of your son.
The best love to come.

48. I Wish

I wish I could share moments with you as I'm
still a kid.

I wish we I could live on Earth with no end.

I wish as the days turn to night I could
see you again.

49. Was Loved

Love.
Loved.
Was love.
Was loved.
An everyday Mother's day
of bliss, and love you was.

50. Understanding

Wisdom.
Understanding.
Love supplied that was in demanding.

51. Crafted

Crafted, and perfected.
Love that was greater than instead of less.
Bless.
Love nest.
Be easy rest.

Love crafted, and perfected.

52. Thanks For

Thanks for the loving.
Extravagent loving far from struggling.

Thanks for the effort.
Loving that didn't get any better.

Thanks for allowing me to be a part of you.
Dream come true.

53. The Will

The way.
The will.
The love the feel.

54. Stages Of Life

Infant.
Childhood.
Adolescence.
Adult.

Live life let your love be felt.

55. Choice

The people's choice.
When around her you must show respect,
lower your voice.

The one that gave life to live.

The lady of love throughout years.

56. A Bliss

Peace and happiness.
Love as a bliss.
An adult that made
Saint Nick Christmas list.

57. Reason To Shine

In love.
In time.
In reason to shine.

In love.
In light.
A delight.

58. An Everday Mother

An everyday Mother's day.
Whip tears away.
Thou shall not go astray.
Cherish the moment, cherish the day
love that shall never ever fade.

59. Lovely As Well

Lovely as well.
Time to reveal.
Inhale, exhale.

Lovely to unveil.
Lovely as well.

60. The Days Of Time

The days of time.
Love all the time.
Love throughout time.
Raising, rising of seeds
to be gentle and kind.

61. The Art Of Love

The art of love.
Her love was showcase it was.
Up above.
Love that floods.
She was, and is love.

62. Such A

Such a loving lady.
Reflection of God, God's baby.

Such a precious lady.

Such different from the others,
loving mother.

63. To Live, Alive

To live.
To be alive.
Live forever in hearts and minds.

64. In Abundance

Abundance.
Lovely, stunning, cunning.
Stood for something.

65. The Love Since Birth

The love since birth.
Love being dispersed.
The greatest love for what it's worth.

66. The Feel

The feel.

The love.

The Grace.

67. I Wish That

I wish that we could live forever,
forever to exist.
You're loved and missed.
Love to it's greatest extent.

68. Time Shared

The time was shared.
Love beyone compared.

Childhood memories,
for all the sweet love
you gave to me.

69. Foremost Love

Foremost.
Love the most.
Love to coast, float.

70. To Become

To become one with the air of surpass the clouds to fly to become.

To become one to shine like the sun.

To become one as eternal life had begun.

71. Love She

Lovely.
Love she.
Love to fly away, be, be free.

72. Version

An added version.
Love deserve.
Love to soar high like the birds.

73. To Lead

To be.
To free.
To see.
To lead.

74. Is Life

Is life.
Paradise.
Reaching perfection of heights.

75. Love, Love

Love, love, love.
Above.
Put no one above.
Dear mother for you I love.

76. Rather

Rather near or far you shine bright like a star.

Trapped in a maze you save.

Daily parades.

Love you gave.

Lovely as the changing of seasons,
enchanting arrays.

77. Love In

Love and opportunity.
Love and unity.
Love and beauty.

78. Trust In

Trust in the power of time.
Make love to me, to my mind.

Trust in the will that be.
Make love to my heart to be free.

79. Champion Love

Champion.
Super woman.
Hero.
Love to grow.

80. At Ease

Degrees.
At ease.
Love she be.
Lovely as can be.
Raised me.
Gave me.
Saved me.

81. Care

Care.
Castle of a layer.
To always be there.
Love that was always there.
Love beyond compare.

82. Love Ordaining

Orchard arrangements.
Substaining.
Remaining.
Gaining.
Love ordaining.

83. To Love Is

To love is to show.

To prepare for the coming events and more.

To enhance becoming a better woman or man.

84. Loved And Blessed

Caress.
Bless.
Love fest.
Loved, and blessed.

85. Love Innovater

Love greater.
Loved previous now and later.
Love innovater.

86. Glowing

Glowing.
Showing.
Growing.

87. Involve

Involve.
Loved all.

Erupt.
Loved very much.

Indulged,
in showing love.

88. Be Uplifted

Be great.
Be gifted.
Be uplifted.

89. Love Without End

A love without end.
A life without sin.
A shoulder to lean a true friend.

90. Desire, Higher

Desire.
Love higher.

To ride.
Glide.
Love to rely.

91. Lovely As They Come

Lovely as they come.

Lovely as healthy new born at birth.

Lovely as the sunrise in the morning
as the birds chirp.

Lovely as love angels being despirsed.

92. Dream Girl

The lover in you.
A dream girl come true.
A female guru.

93. Lady Be Free

Be free.
Be thee.
Lovely lady be free.

94. A Formality

In love.

In vitality.

In pleasure as a formality.

95. We Live, We Perish

We live, we perish.
Love and marriage.
We give, we gave, love made.

96. Was Pleasant

In time was pleasant.
A gift, a present.
Precious.

97. Relief

Relief.
Belief.
Love deep.

98. Of Time

Signs of time.
Love in time.
Shine in time.
Live forever in time.

99. Take flight

The love of life.
To fly to take flight.
Paradise.

100. Select

Select.
Love without reject.
No upset.
Cool breeze, without sweat.
Love as the best it gets.

Printed in the United States
by Baker & Taylor Publisher Services